Everything Has Been Asking For Mercy

poems by

Ginna Luck

Finishing Line Press
Georgetown, Kentucky

Everything Has Been Asking For Mercy

ACKNOWLEDGMENTS

Publisher: Leah Maines
Editor: Christen Kincaid
Cover Art: Richard Luck
Author Photo: Richard Luck
Cover Design: Elizabeth Maines McCleavy

Printed in the USA on acid-free paper.
Order online: www.finishinglinepress.com
also available on amazon.com

Author inquiries and mail orders:
Finishing Line Press
P. O. Box 1626
Georgetown, Kentucky 40324
U. S. A.

Table of Contents

Snow...1

Recovery 2

Don't Wonder don't Share 4

Onset of Illness 5

There is Too Much of a Dead Thing in Me 7

One Hundred Yards 8

No Summer 10

The Milk on the Shelf Remains the Milk on the Shelf....11

The Sky Turned Red..13

There Is No Space Here For Waiting...............................16

I Gave You No Answer...19

Dream Funeral...20

Everything Has Been Asking For Mercy.........................22

And Here I Am Crying Over The Darkness of My
Own Pocket...24

Little Blister Slit of a Heart...25

It Hurts To Not Be What I am 26

Self Portrait With White Buttons 27

Something In Me Just Sits There Like A Backpack Full
of Nonperishable Food Stuff...28

Do You See Anything Beautiful In This?..31

There Has Never Been So Many Waste Bins, So Many
Banged Out Old Garbage Lids...33

Brambles 35

The Desert 36

To Make It Make Sense..37

Will I Ever See You Again..39

The Good Body...41

Note To Self..43

Damn That Embarrassing So Sick World Of No Human
Power You've Come From 46

Get Up Dummy, Get Up..47

In The Hour Of My Own Undoing 49

I Must Assume Many Things If I'm Going To Wear
You Down 51

I Choke Silence From The Soft Joints Of Poems 54

My Whole Life I Am Afraid And Then I Die..................................56

Finally, You Realize How To Turn Off The Alarm 59

I Can Arrive For You...60

Author Bio...63

For Richard

Snow

I've walked for hours in the dark to arrive miles away in the snow.

The snow that pressed to my mouth like a wound and I couldn't feel.

I couldn't feel my lips or fingers while the night around me wept.

While it wept through the tall pines for something I knew before.

Before it all moved into my open hands then dissolved like snow.

I've walked for hours to arrive like a night with no barriers but snow.

The snow how it felt like my thoughts that I couldn't get through.

Get through and into a pattern like day and night day and surrender.

The surrender of trees, snow and blood, moonlight and the rest of it.

The surrender of distance cut into smaller pieces melting a little more.

A little more every day in the dark and angry wind whipping up the snow.

I've walked for hours calling out to myself in the dark to come home.

Come home to the self I knew before everything was covered in snow.

The snow that pressed to my mouth like the truth and I couldn't feel.

I couldn't feel the slow hours moving toward me and eager to touch.

To touch my fingertips and lips like anything alive and trying to live.

Trying to live a little longer in the world on skin and inside my mouth.

My mouth split from the dead trees on the hills that are covered in snow.

The snow that pressed to my mouth like a wound and I couldn't feel.

Recovery

I thought I shouldn't listen to the incessant demands of my body.

I thought my hunger was the hollow sky I was in love with.

I wanted to feel

my hip bones like their own perfect story

glowing of my brilliant control.

I wanted to close my teeth

on my continuing discomfort,

uncurl into a ghost that wandered out of myself

and into whatever else was comfortable in the dust

like more dust in a column of dusty light

coming down on me in a mindless grimy sunset.

I was caught in its ridiculous hands, alive only in its fingers.

I'm talking about denial

so complete, its loss became an unplaceable thing inside me.

An unknowable vessel.

A fifty-pound block of my own beefed-up pain,

fat and ripe like a dead

horse's thick, sun crusted meat. Everything moved

ahead in small unequal pieces and outward in every direction.

And although there was nothing left for me to see,

I kept seeing all that was not actually there:

what I'd always had becoming

the thing I'd lost slowly repeating on the ground next to me, again.

The stranger I saw looking back through the mirror was a child

who could barely

speak, whose face was covered in brambles,

and not just covered, tangled over and through, unable,

at last, to pretend there was anything else happening.

Don't Wonder, Don't Share

A tightened loop rings my smashed purple skin, makes the things I feel seem less real all stupid inside and punched clean of a story. I thought I was busy repairing a decimated forest or was it a little boat, its searchlights? I can't remember and it doesn't really matter. Millions of different things turned out to be just one thing happening over and over, and what a trick it was to wrap myself into a paralyzing knot and think I could live like that forever and we could all be friends and laugh.

Onset Of Illness

I hear my lungs

filling and emptying

the smallest flutter

of mosquitoes.

I watch my knees

crush a busted chair.

My fingers go numb

then my arm up to my elbow.

I don't remember falling

inside the mind of another person

maybe even someone dead.

I do remember a dark eyed

girl, seven or eight

that could not stop vomiting.

The paramedic's hands

feel leathery like garlic cloves.

I desperately want to grow

into the little girl's bony elbows.

I wonder how my hands

can go so limp and bloodless

a dark hole of muddy water by the coat stand.

There is Too Much of a Dead Thing in Me

The dead thing cannot speak and so it is chipping away at some dried up paint and dust to make the words. The words are loamy and soaking and can't be seen. The words are sinking between the sidewalk stones and further down beneath the dirt and crumbling into an inarticulable strangeness. The dead thing is bringing my face closer to the strangeness, is stealing my head so I can be alone with the strangeness. Everything I say sounds like gravel then nothing then a series of opening and shutting doors. I feel a muscly piece of a shattered wing in my hand. I feel the feeling of my blood running through a greenish tunnel. I see the tooth marks. I see the scratches and the divots. I see a life of another's choosing. And always I am hanging on to the lost things snagged on a branch. A sliver of mirk sticks to my knuckles in the dark and says nothing. A branch is covered with a thousand big-eyed bugs. What is it that I've lost? The dead thing never quite remembers. The dead thing is so full of people who don't know who they are. Maybe I'm not one of the people I am? A white liquid is bleeding all over. There are so many entrances to nowhere that my mind wants to burst.

One Hundred Yards

I am sick again

blotted out between the bed sheets

smoothed over and floral printed.

A never laundered towel hangs

on the post at my feet.

It is a normal Monday.

The throb of street lights kick in my ears

and rain drips from the gutters. I cannot walk

my kids the one hundred yards

to the bus stop anymore

and I do not know how to tolerate

the end the things.

I crack my window.

Cold air touches the dip

between my collarbone and neck

where the skin is the thinnest

where it seems like death

is very possible.

So much has slipped out and into silt mirk.

I feel myself looking for myself

and I am looking at the back of the sofa

and then a chair comes into view.

I've lost unidentified periods of time

waiting to wake up each morning lifted

by the smallest push inside me.

I touch my throat to feel

for a pulse and a little brown bat

is there sleeping

down in my papery skin.

I've tried so many ways to save things.

No Summer

So, it is summer, maybe. I don't know.

The sunlight clumps.

Hours circle big as bombs.

I'm so stuffed up

with demons today

I sting for the green rot

in rain, the moss along bright

dead, dotted stumps

a different soft green

that whines

to be touched.

A hummingbird

pauses above me, sucks

glass. The past is so fat.

Who have I been

outside of holding my breath? Every day

I must live in a terrified map of pins.

The Milk on the Shelf Remains the Milk on the Shelf

The store is not far from my home.

The milk is just one item

between the cheese and the sour cream.

My sickness cannot be seen

beyond my mind, good and stalled

cannot be pulled from its block, that little rock

how my skin takes it into the bulk, shrinks

it to water and salt. I know I do it wrong

smother the mouth of every joy

and shuttle brainlessly

to the store. I tell myself it's brave

to lose the thing that cannot be lost. So watch me

reach the end of worry

rattle myself off of this gloom route

gather my form to send it forward. Push it

my skin, those dammed, doomed organs.

Another day, another box. Push it

to the ground

with the quiet small critters

who burrow in the dirt

the still sleeping beetles

the living who live in the world like air in air

the forgettable dark quiet non-experience

let it last forever. I too am blessed

with the ability to not think that much.

Buy the milk, think buy the milk. I have a job to do, so I do it.

And above, the sun expands like loose skin, throbbing

like a cut-up head. And look there is blood

on the street from the dying animals, look at it tearing loose

from a tree like an overripe fruit. Look at its almost-life

pressing the bad spot in my brain.

I understand the brutality of endurance

but how about the body

and the boat of hope or the forgive me

while I sleep,

the four-sided mirror of mercy,

what about that?

The Sky Turned Red

A sound is made

when everything

inside grows

lighter and lighter

when in

the world

and then into

more a stranger

in a world

I failed

to imagine

without you

your silence

is a sound

off the back

of your head

my hands

are there

to unhurt it

as not

to leave it

to sorrow

there is enough

sorrow

in leaving

there is enough

sorrow

in a sunset

a light

that marks the world

for departure

it is far too easy

to come apart

to fall

beneath the things

we are meant

to climb over

we are more

sky than we are

bone

we are affected

by the moon

I can't blame you

for the brevity

of things

the loss

of life is flickering

under our feet

you bend down

and kiss the sand

if you could love me

more easily

you would love

me more easily

There Is No Space Here For Waiting

In a narrow room with one tired window

is my heart on my arm like a complicated feeling.

In a narrow room with one tired window

is a bed made from a spot

on my face

that looks like

old age

and I have to lie down

on it anyway.

In a narrow room with one tired

window is a broken

box

of hours

I can't do anything

with, my invisible life

lit up all over the walls

I am thinking of where life happens

and a single frozen shoe

like a dead bird drags

from my mouth.

I am thinking of my family

and tall weeds grow

out of a love note.

I am thinking of one room full

of windows and a hole

in my tooth

becomes one

very

radiant

light.

And outside the window falls the rain.

And outside the window is an unfinished

sky between my children's open arms.

I have no idea of the distances.

I slide the window open and open.

The rain is warm.

Why not just accept it.

I Gave You No Answer

I drew my sickness in a circle on your chest and lit the circle on fire.

I draped my body over you like a dense green moss.

The fire was more than our anatomy.

My sickness was more than the fire.

The fire breathed like a room full of people clutching and kissing wide mouthed.

The fire spit blue pulse of sparks into our hot empty mouths.

Our mouths became a flaming hoop brighter than every volcano.

A tight circle of green became tragically powerful.

I saw how my sickness made you uncomfortable.

Dream Funeral

I am on an island with everyone I've ever loved or wanted to love that hasn't loved me back. I spend all day wanting something warm in my hand. Where there should be my lover's mouth, there is the mindless humming sound of the ocean. Where there should be my lover's eyes, there is salt etched into the groves of my skin. A faceless face is pressed to my ear like splattered blood. I want the faceless face to love me. I want the faceless face to be so empty I can fit in. I can live in the cave of the faceless face, dig a hole into teeth and lips and save at least one of us. I am so sick for love to emerge in the cold sea. For it to tug and tug through the soft sucking mud into the strange spot on my humiliating heart. People often disappear. They are the most beautiful right before they're gone. They are something else: a double rainbow, an optical phenomena that brings me back to my invisible, violent love each time. I miss my love the most of all. I miss believing in something I can't see. I am so sad for the luminous to say I love you. For the musical pain to puff up in my sore heart holes. With all the beauty dead how will

I cry for your hands? Where are the burning trees, the stinging blood moon? There is no way to love each other. I want to get up but I don't know where to walk where I won't run into an ocean. I don't want to walk through an ocean.

Everything Has Been Asking For Mercy

There is no grace left in black water. It has lost everything electric. When I tell you I can't do this anymore, I am actually telling you I am a river at the place it meets the sea.

I am speed and depth and escaping. I am water and the length it takes to travel from here to anywhere and I can't ocean myself anymore. Grief has tiny fish bones that splinter in wave over wave over whomever I love. I want to think about the sky.

I want to think about light splitting at the edge of darkness like ribbons of silk. I want to see the storm coming and a bolt of lightning strike a cliff. I want the cliff to explode go howling into flames and remind me I'm capable of love. I can love you

as light waves. I can love you like resin and hot air against the curve of your arm. Think about light preservation and then these words and then nothing at all. I want to step out of language and into a tall grass field on fire and watch the flames gnaw through so much dirt. Think about whirlpools and then light traps and especially moths. Think about a sky electric with what you don't have.

I don't have to be my most difficult dream.

I want to extinguish the dream and put your body in its place. There is stillness at the core of any explosion. I think we can be that stillness.

And Here I Am Crying Over The Darkness Of My Own Pocket

My desire is a different sun going down and down and I too am falling pulled and curled to the shape of the earth disappearing or already gone. Don't say tomorrow. Don't climb to the edge of a cliff and look out. I've placed the horizon deep into a small hole with my hands, made and remade a hundred times just to see what is done to the under air. Nothing is ever diminished. Remember me slipping out of your arms. Remember my body like the heat that leaves your breath. Imagine my arms as some dying language and the afterglow is I and I am the indefinite sky, how I open and open like a mouth with no sound, my skin half full of smoke and sundown. See how there is no light and only rain like a billion pleas for forgiveness, all the quiet trying hard to break away into living. It is almost like touching.

Little Blister Slit of a Heart

My therapist confirms for me today that I have a strong need

to be liked and I'm anxious

to please. I am who I am

only in private

and even then it is difficult

to know if the ground is soft

or if it is loaded with rocks. I mean I am unsure

of the floorboards

creaking over there, if I am in the kitchen

or against the light of my mother's face.

I will always be lousy at dancing.

I've spent hours and months trying

to make myself small

and that is no place to spin

or think about a dance floor or the hips

of strangers.

It Hurts To Not Be What I Am

I live in an orphan vessel. I freeze to death in a flimsy theater again in the box bitten by strange and anxious winks. I have tiny blood. I hush up in the scared bucket. The cold, the heat. I'm on my knees stamped into plastic looks. I am not in the sure. I don't even know what I know. (This too is work.) I have many empty stings. I die a little on language. The part that is bearable is also false. My origin shoulder punishes me. I swamp in the acid of yesterday. I pull at the edges until I see blood. I stand knee-deep in useless soul leaves. I tongue shock quiet. I punch tenderness. I slam on toward love. I ring through the meanest direction. I gleam my lowest habit. I slip on my shame blanket. I beat back deep humiliation. I mother what threatens the peace in the blackout. What could burst could be anything. I cannot body future. I cannot flesh it up.

Self Portrait With White Buttons

I stand in front of the mirror. What I see is the skin between the bottom of my shirt and the top of my jeans. What I see are my hips through thin clothing and my hipbones and anger. The fabric is fraying all over. What I see is the small vertical cleft between the tip of my nose and the top of my upper lip. What I see are my sleeves smallish and unacknowledged. I get the feeling I am eating them inside my skull. I spit out static and fluff and try not think about my heart in the world instead of my shoes. What's next: the dry skin on the inside of my thigh. I cannot see it, but it hurts me now as does the rough bottoms of my feet. I think I will buy new socks. What I see is my personal pain in my loose fitted undershirt. I feel it might snag or rip or injure me. I undress. There must be no self-pity. I want an outfit that does not say how I am feeling, something I can look at and not see absolute powerlessness. I put on the legs and weight of my smallest emotion. I proceed forward but nothing changes.

Something In Me Just Sits There Like a Backpack Full of Nonperishable Food Stuff

I want to feel my personality dropped through space.

I want to undress in the dark and cover myself back up again

with the want and vanish I've been dreaming of for years.

I will create nothing. Teach myself I am capable

of nothing. Nothing is what I am after. Emptiness

is the valley where I live. I don't want

to be good. I want to curl up

in a cloud cubicle soft as an eyelid and snore

the sky pulled down around my head.

And god, how I need its mindless grimy sunset drowned

at the bottom of my belly, glowy and blurred.

My ears covered with cold gravity

and punctured by the sharpened teeth of trees.

No noise inside my body but the leaking

red-orange feeling of atmospheric light.

This makes me feel more

normal and lovable, pretty even, like some cloud

or soft other place, happy

with what can't be: the perfect body-shape

to go forward, to be seen. I am instinctively afraid

of looking inward, which is to say I forget

the language of my body.

What I think is the rising sun

is a long and difficult disease.

What I think is the green, perfectly

manicured lawn is the midnight light

spilling across a tiny plate. Everyone I love

is falling from the sky into a terrifying forest.

The earth comes to my door

with only meat and hair.

I search its insides

and find two years dead face down in a bulge

of blue smoke. I am so hungry

all the time hungry for my hands

in the air forever. I eat all the sky

I can find, hiding and crying

and eating in the dark for hours the black

bulkiest air of my life.

Oh god, a little glowing soundwave

in the dirt-bright silence.

I open my mouth.

I swallow a rockslide.

The meteor shower goes on pummeling.

Do You See Anything Beautiful In This?

There is only one color on the earth with all of its parts separate spread out on the grass like marbles. I am not so complicated and that's okay.

Sometimes I need fewer choices—you dumb animal.

Consider instead, the buzzing shimmering quadrant of energy in my mouth, how quiet it actually is. The question is whether or not to be kind to the silence.

Some things happen in the grass. The sun is as dangerous as ever. The sky is so ambitious. The lilacs are sprouting out of a pipe in the wall. There are so many ways to be sick.

I find all the ways and float lazily on through their elaborate tunnels, move dirt into my unconscious and wait for you in my pain body.

Have we fallen into my loneliness or are we very much in love? Don't make me choose. They are both so pretty.

A fly gets stuck in language and sad blooms into a sink of headaches. I wash my hair with a sick person and lots of ideas get lost.

Wrap your lips around my sadness spectacle and blink into the same dark complex as mine. Oh, you burning little body clamped onto my disappearing project, thank you. I was worried I'd hurt alone.

Let's go out into the center of things wearing my imaginary crown and making new noises. Let's pretend the dirt is nothing on my knees. I can stay confident in my ability to scrape the sick from my body and fling it out into the stones!

A welt appears on my arm. I taste a little blood in my mouth. Some things I just can't do.

There Has Never Been So Many Waste Bins, So Many Banged Out Old Garbage Lids

I ask you to love me and then work every hour toward a feeling of insufficiency so complete it becomes a city of spectacular buildings: a spire about to explode in the sunset, a steal skeleton refracting like an electric dancer, sky-scraped and bleached with lightening. You enter expecting magic to happen and instead a deformed tower rises up in a car lot.

I ask you to love me and then dangle your heart outside an apartment complex like toilet paper aorta smeared and sick with its own pain seeping through a greasy curtain. Another dead condo is about to be toppled cracked, hemorrhaging out a skylight. My clavicle is caving in.

I ask you to love me helplessly from a place of weakness from the ground torn to dirt so there is no steady place to stand. Stay with me. Stay only with me. Stay in the overturned earth and metal of a dead year. In a city that broke up and out of my hands like a cage of cracked lights.

There is always a fire alarm blaring under my skin. Always industrialized landscapes up ahead somewhere, machines building new machines building a duplex forest of waste and more waste that can't be kept. The problem is this is

not a city that stops.

Brambles

If I plant a garden I will plant only brambles that grow even when it is not spring because I am afraid of dying I will dig into the earth and plant rows and rows of them though they are not beautiful though they are not something we can love we will always be children there the air soft as dough flipping the dark leaves over but then I start thinking of blossoms and the bright desert.

The Desert

I arrive in the middle of a desert made entirely of my skin blown through the high, cold atmosphere and thrown down as dirt and dust and wind-blown sand. Thick clouds of heat move like hollow bodies opening and re-opening to the light of a thunderstorm burned into red mountainous rocks. I strike a match and set fire to a tree. The branches curl up and explode in the air like a live star, the flames thick and too hot snap light against the sky and create ten thousand sunsets. Yes, there is all this absurd beauty. From out of my arms ash and smoke blow freely, curl up into a hand that waves and then breaks across a desert of my skin and into some naked and howling future. I've never really seen anyone die.

To Make It Make Sense

I am seeing it the way I can only see it when I am a mile over, a year over, a decade over, a whole sky over my same sick body

looks so small and so beautifully alien from way up here, all mud no wounds, my ideas and thoughts threading outside into one small mess of land and consciousness and whatever it is I thought I feared: the restless, changeable tundra? It continues to move

continues to rock and pulse and breathe. Hard grains of sand turn from objects to animals into something else that asks again and again if it can be made new because it can no longer endure its shape.

The throngs of trees have chopped themselves down and what's left are the flies all over the green ground dying to show me the truth about some version of myself but I can't tell what that version is.

I don't even remember the stupid things I did and why I took them into me, stone by stone gathering up into black hills. Crows fluttering in my veins.

What I do remember is the weakening shape of my body becoming nothing I can recognize. What I do remember is losing the dark trees in the landscape through the tiny window, the heart not even the heart.

I can't accurately perceive things on the ground. What sound goes with what color, what light goes with what thought patterns, what feelings go with what smashed up field or forest, which is only pasture and stink and mushrooms and rotting leaves. Everything absorbs into the color of grass.

Will I Ever See You Again

I found a strange animal. I found it wounded in the grass. I brought it home. I let it sleep in my bed on my pillow. I don't like a thing to be lonely. I fed it from my hand. I held its tiny black mouth up to my ear. I listened to its magnetic apparatus. I listened all day, all night. I loosened up its sounds with my tongue. I sanded its belly smooth enough to fit in its wires. I welcomed its whirlwind under my covers. The invisible and also the rubble (which seemed to be a symptom of the hard weather). It had the most beautiful eyes. Eyes like the surface of the ocean, huge and crashing, almost white. The most scoured and icy of eyes. And no, no I was not afraid. Even as its fur smoked off its translucent, spiny legs. Even as I could see its skeleton sliver out from its skin like a pothole, I called it onto my flesh. It crawled up my arm and clung to my hair. It slipped, without sound, backward into my chest and stayed for years within my channels. I could write my name but that was all. It moved and I moved. It thought and I said: *all things will be heavy*, and they were. I heard them stomping even in my sleep. A hissing pollution filled my hands. Every noise stung a different ghost or a clump of hair or something in place of the animal I had taken into my body—its claws slowly pulling out, its startled, dark stump escaping. Its black tongue clicked into never. Even my breathing left a cold space you couldn't even open. You didn't even try. It wasn't good to slip

into.

The Good Body

I can shape myself perfectly into the hum of florescent lights. I can sit so still the minutes part dark and slow and deep through me like a small animal's scream vibrates all night through a blue spruce. I can press my body down into the space where I don't know anything but the deadly weight of all my imagined doom. And there, at the bottom of the world, living creatures spin and splinter and fight.

They walk with their eyes shut and see with their fingers. They stick their hands into sewers and caverns and slip in the moon. They thrive in shadow. They contort into its pale blue frailty. They muscle themselves into nothing but silver and silence—windblown and cloud like. They laugh. They laugh and laugh and laugh at my daily rituals of resistance. At my inability to see further than only a couple inches. At my rigid, embittered carefulness.

They laugh at a world that has me in its grip like a gangly girl. Small, easy to forget a sad-boned thing. And I am retreating into my sadness like a tiny particle of dust cries downward into a ditch. What should I do with my hands? I am not a wise traveler. Please teach me, simple creatures, what to do with my available body.

Bring your war against my present complaints. Every sorry edged thought, put its tiny scull in your pocket. Carve out a truer, purer god from my permeant defeat. Make me so fierce and bright in all my injuries. I can't think of anything else I could want that could be so important.

Get Up Dummy, Get Up

The old shit you can't forget slow swirls out a forgotten window in the back wall of your skull and a flurry of dark winged creatures escapes from the cave of your gut.

They scream or cry or whatever their grossed out inky black faces love to do in your body, but this time through windows, coming in also through doors, and every opening, even the ones you cannot see.

In any other house they would have penetrated everything: walls and ripped sheets and bookshelves, dragged their jaws through every stone and brick in the dark of the basement; jabbed their tongues through key holes and gutters and underfloor crawl spaces, screaming out electrical outlets and water pipes: heads that feed on dead skin and your blind as a bat worrying.

But instead, upon entering, their legs disintegrate into small bumps on their abdomens. Most of them are missing their wings. Black splotches stumble along white crown molding. If you tap your fingers lightly on the floorboards, their little spiny bodies scurry into non-existence or get sucked up into nothing but a pile of dishtowels on the floor. Small enough for you to fend away with one hand. Or not, since there is space for them here and they won't linger

regardless. There is nothing to eat.

In The Hour Of My Own Undoing

"Spirit rules secretly alone the body achieves nothing is something you know."
—Anne Carson

I will cultivate a mile of green grass in the early summer rain. I will shake fog into a forest at night like someone who left and then returns for love. If love seems emptier still, I will remind you, even silence flourishes. If you listen closely

you'll hear the slow sinking moon and all the dead light ready to disappear. I will disappear. I will die and be reborn a tree. What will pulse inside me will not be a heart, but a broken and upended oak branch that heaves and sunders and grinds into beautiful slick pink underneath. I will crush you

with the promise of lushness. I'll be more like any shade of the color green, everything that seems to grow and grow. You can run your hands through the moss and feel a vein, a gash, where broken skin knits together and sprouts viable and green. Push your heart into it like a muddied boot print.

Dig a hole in it and get to know me again. I am composing a new blood you can breathe. I am writing this poem inside of you. A new line appears in your palm. Every now and then we touch and something drops from the sky: moths

or bees and small bird bodies. I see three thousand miles of water before us

and nothing

but tiny green frogs skating over it. What I'm trying to say is, the more loss there

is, the more I will wash myself into new shapes. I have unthinkable hugeness if

a whole lot of my thinking can change. Everything that is difficult becomes a

system of transformation. At the end of the day, I have to stop being so fearful.

I Must Assume Many Things If I'm Going To Wear You Down

What a dull little bird you are

a dull little thing, afraid to move, afraid

of your body, your soft beak, your subtle feet,

your tiny black head.

Little bird, you've already lost

your world and here you are continuing

in my hands as bone and feather

a hot burn of beak and claw

into my blank flesh.

I'll admit that I am scared

that I only remember

what it feels like to hurt

and be hurt

that some mornings I find

myself a hollow boned bird

roughed winged swallow banged

against the window.

Why do you flap yourself raw

and meaningless when you cannot fly?

Why do you fight beneath all that difficulty?

I don't want you, little bird.

I don't want to keep going

the way you've been going

all through the air, the sky

stiffening up like a bad limb

like a broken and damn near dead bird.

Close your black beak.

Where there is just your rough grackle

I will call it my beautiful park

with my neighborhood song bird.

Our bodies may be indistinguishable

but I am not actually walking

in circular hobbles

dragging a wing through a puddle

of grease or huddled down

in one tiny swath of grass like defenseless

eggs. I am sitting in the dirt without

making my mind aware of the dirt.

I am allowing the invisible stuff to move

my mouth and take my bleeding chin.

My face forgetting my face

on a bus or a train sometimes a bicycle.

The solution looks like you

because it is you:

the worst of all things

is actually what keeps

this circus train moving.

I Choke Silence from the Soft Joints of Poems

and diffuse it

until it becomes the black

all around and inside

and the space it fills and keeps trying to fill

and still I do not give in.

I believe in language

the way sensation fingers through

it like small remnants of teeth

over an unclosed wound.

I lean my face into the wind

and start to believe

it's a smoldering pit

cooled by the breath of an animal

a million miles away that I was meant to swallow.

I feel the knuckles of its spine

rise up like a staircase to climb.

I cross great seas of flesh

with no more than a blood-flecked voice

the word forsaken sweating from my palms an ocean

and here it comes: one more wave moving

around me and within and all the dirt that lays beneath.

I drag my tongue like a rotting fish

across it, lick up

the ruined words

so filling my chest

I think I might never

have to breathe again.

My Whole Life I Am Afraid and Then I Die

Once I saw a bright mouth

a light orange and white

from its lips

this low humming light

visible like smoke

a smoke cloud drifting

inside an arm

ricocheting off a wrist

and wiping everything out.

Even what the mouth had said.

Even how it loved

eating away all the fat

and leaving

the body transparent.

It was the most beautiful moment

as if I stood outside the skin

of our collapsed love.

I wept and screamed

and that's when a black

flower lifted off like a dress

flayed open in the wind

weightless bloodless.

There was nothing to hold anything down.

Hands and faces

everything suddenly became unstuck

floated off into the day

and day went dark.

It just fizzed and got dark

this warm aromatic dark

a lingering smell of rain and flesh

becoming something that never loved

never could have loved

much simpler, much easier

to understand nothing

but thin translucent sound

nothing but vibration

something fragile again

arriving softly

all the sorrow gone out.

Finally, You Realize How To Turn Off The Alarm

So, sit down. Have a drink. Take it in the Jacuzzi in the dark. Soak up to your neck and close your eyes and dream of the wrinkling flesh at the base of your heel. Dream of your toes sleek as a dolphins, your toes like strange looking water fountains, your toes like white baskets on a windowsill. Dream of your dumb feet.

Wake up simple with some space around your head. You are here for new ideas. Imagine busting out of your birthday cake angle-faced and laughing, your jiggling belly exposed in all its smeared sweat and salty fat. You are beginning. Just beginning to run through unknown rooms with your eyes closed.

You smash into a side table and shake off like a peacock. Everything falls from your pockets: dollars and coins, clumps of hair, something like a wing and a buzzing, yellow little mouth that can gnaw down a finger.

Turns out the terrible sickness that was trying to get you was in your pockets not your bloodstream. So here's a vacation, a hundred dollars, an inventive child. Stuff it all in where it won't fall out. Blindness and vulnerability are in your living room, so why not learn to play the saxophone.

I Can Arrive For You

Today I take note of the trees

and the blossoms on the trees without thinking of dying.

When I see a woman wiping the mouth of her child

and then hurrying to the bus

I think I am just like her.

Every longing isn't lined with pain.

Every ache isn't an ache for myself.

I am anyone: the girl sitting on her hands

in front of the Shell station

the man steaming shirts at the dry cleaner

the stranger

I recognize the smell of

the woman who keeps to herself.

I rest, I work, I hurry forward

to what I will become.

My future is not a long distance call

tumbling in static but here now

open, really open, like something young

coming together and reaching out.

For the first time in months

I love what is right in front of me

the lead sky, the old rain in the gutter like rotten fruit.

There doesn't need to be great distance.

When I think about God

I think of how things transform. A huge stonewall

in the middle of the night

is an open field by morning.

And when the rain comes

and it always comes, dark as the wind

in the belly of the sky and loud as glass

splintering through trees, hissing

like a heavy, black arrow

I will pull my name back.

I will carry it out in front of me

and give it to anyone

cold and wet and in the middle of sorry

sorry for everything so ugly.

I am done being afraid.

I am done with sadness

like a fake moon

all the time out my window.

I can love someone who is not dissolving into the horizon.

After ten years of disordered eating, anxiety and depression, at twenty six years old, **Ginna Luck** was diagnosed with chronic fatigue, also known as myalgic encephalomyelitis or M.E. At thirty, after the birth of her second child, the illness became too severe for her to work. She stayed mostly at home for the next nine years concentrating on her writing and raising her boys. Still ill with chronic fatigue, she was able to attend a low residency MFA program at Goddard College in Port Townsend, WA, where she studied fiction. Two years after her graduation, in the start of 2015, she began writing the poetry collection: *Everything Has Been Asking For Mercy*. Her work can be read in *Radar Poetry, Gone Lawn, decomP, Hermeneutic Chaos Journal, Bodega, Rust + Moth, Leveler Poetry, Up the Staircase Quarterly* and elsewhere. She has been nominated for two Pushcart Prizes.

www.ingramcontent.com/pod-product-compliance
Lightning Source LLC
Chambersburg PA
CBHW021201090426
42740CB00008B/1187